Dat

# Table tennis 10 and 1

## Recognise the place value of each digit in a 2-digit number

3   8

7   2

☐ has ☐ 10s and ☐ 1s.
☐ has ☐ 10s and ☐ 1s.

☐ has ☐ 10s and ☐ 1s.
☐ has ☐ 10s and ☐ 1s.

5   1

4   9

☐ has ☐ 10s and ☐ 1s.
☐ has ☐ 10s and ☐ 1s.

☐ has ☐ 10s and ☐ 1s.
☐ has ☐ 10s and ☐ 1s.

### Teacher's notes

Children look at the numbers on each pair of table tennis bats and use them to make two, two-digit numbers. They write these on the table tennis balls. Then they complete each of the sentences underneath to identify the tens and ones digits in each number.

**Date:** _____

# Sort the orders!

Order numbers to 100 and use the <, > and = signs

| 14 | = | 48 | 23 | > | 14 |

○ ○ ○
○ ○ ○

| 37 | < | = | 26 | 19 | 26 |

○ ○ ○
○ ○ ○

| > | 62 | 59 | < | 43 | 43 |

○ ○ ○
○ ○ ○

| 81 | = | 78 | 90 | < | 90 |

○ ○ ○
○ ○ ○

**Teacher's notes**

Children look at the numbers and symbols on the trays that the waiters are carrying. They then rearrange these into two statements, each with two numbers and a symbol, and write these onto the plates.

4

# Collins

Busy Ant Maths

# Activity Book 2C

Date: _____

# Caterpillar 3s

## Count in steps of 3

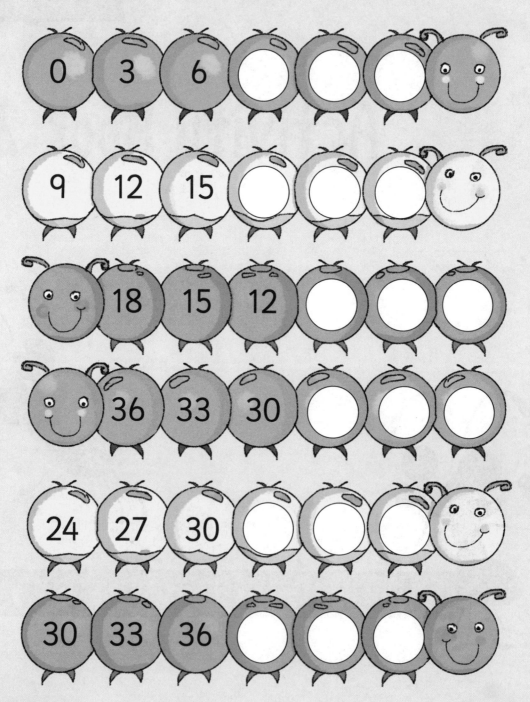

**Teacher's notes**

Children count on or back in steps of three and write the missing numbers onto each caterpillar.

Date: _____

# Rocket routes and space steps

## Solve problems about place value

0 — 2 — ☐ — ☐ — ☐ — 20

0 — 3 — ☐ — ☐ — ☐ — 30

| 5 | | |
|---|---|---|
| | 16 | |
| 25 | | 28 |

| 33 | | |
|---|---|---|
| | | 44 |
| 51 | 53 | |

| | | |
|---|---|---|
| 67 | | 69 |
| | | 80 |

| | 83 | |
|---|---|---|
| | | 95 |

**Teacher's notes**

At the top of the page, children write the correct number on each blank star in the number lines, counting in twos for the first row, and in threes for the second row. At the bottom of the page, they complete each set of steps by writing in the boxes the missing numbers. Each set of space launch steps is part of a 1–100 number square.

Date: _____

# Apple addition

## Add two 2-digit numbers

**You will need:**
- 1–100 number square

14 + 25 = ☐

31 + 17 = ☐

26 + 23 = ☐

13 + 42 = ☐

32 + 54 = ☐

75 + 22 = ☐

18 + 26 = ☐

28 + 35 = ☐

47 + 15 = ☐

38 + 43 = ☐

27 + 64 = ☐

76 + 16 = ☐

## Teacher's notes

Children use a 1–100 number square to help them add each pair of two-digit numbers.

Date: _____

# Kangaroo addition

## Add two 2-digit numbers

$12 + 25 =$ 37

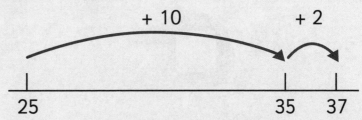

$34 + 24 =$ ☐

$37 + 42 =$ ☐

$16 + 27 =$ ☐

$46 + 28 =$ ☐

$39 + 55 =$ ☐

**Teacher's notes**

Children use the number line beside each calculation to help them work out the answer.

Date: _____

# Snail subtraction

Subtract two 2-digit numbers

**You will need:**
• 1–100 number square

25 – 14 =

37 – 23 =

48 – 21 =

56 – 35 =

79 – 57 =

87 – 66 =

34 – 19 =

45 – 27 =

51 – 15 =

63 – 38 =

76 – 49 =

92 – 65 =

**Teacher's notes**

Children use a 1–100 number square to help them subtract each pair of two-digit numbers.

Date: _____

# Frog subtraction

## Subtract two 2-digit numbers

$26 - 14 =$ 12

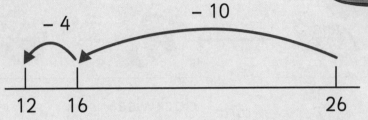

$$- 4 \qquad - 10$$

12    16          26

$38 - 25 =$ ☐

$49 - 17 =$ ☐

$34 - 18 =$ ☐

$52 - 25 =$ ☐

$73 - 47 =$ ☐

**Teacher's notes**

Children use the number line beside each calculation to help them work out the answer.

9

# Turn, turn, turn

## Recognise size and direction of turn

| $\frac{1}{4}$ | turn | clockwise |
|---|---|---|
| | or | |
| $\frac{3}{4}$ | turn | anti-clockwise |

| | turn | |
|---|---|---|
| | or | |
| | turn | |

| | turn | |
|---|---|---|
| | or | |
| | turn | |

| | turn | |
|---|---|---|
| | or | |
| | turn | |

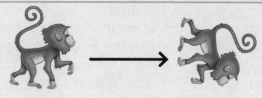

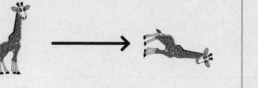 

| | turn | |
|---|---|---|
| | or | |
| | turn | |

| | turn | |
|---|---|---|
| | or | |
| | turn | |

### Teacher's notes

Children identify the amount of turn and the direction of turn for each animal, expressing each turn in both directions: clockwise and anti-clockwise.

# Through the key hole?

**Date:** _____

## Recognise a right angle

| Start | | | | |

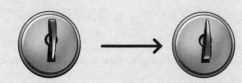

_____ right angle turns

_____ right angle turns

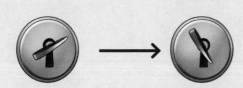

_____ right angle turns

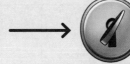

_____ right angle turns

### Teacher's notes

At the top of the page, children look at the first key and decide whether each of the four keys beside it is now at right angles from their starting position. They put a tick or cross in the box to indicate 'yes' or 'no'. At the bottom of the page, for each pair of keys children write the number of right angles that the key has turned.

Date: _____

# Snow maze

## Follow and write directions

**You will need:**
- two different coloured pencils

| Start | | | | | 🌲 | | 🌲 | 🌲 | 🌲 |
|---|---|---|---|---|---|---|---|---|---|
| | 🌲 | 🌲 | 🌲 | | 🌲 | 🌲 | | 🌲 | |
| | 🌲 | 🌲 | 🌲 | | 🌲 | 🌲 | | | |
| | | | | | | | | 🌲 | |
| | | 🌲 | 🌲 | 🌲 | 🌲 | 🌲 | 🌲 | | 🏁 |

**Snowboarder A**

Go forward 4 squares
Make 1 right angle turn clockwise.
Go forward 3 squares.
Make 1 right angle turn clockwise.
Go forward 3 squares.
Make 1 **right angle turn anticlockwise**.
Go forward 1 square.

**Snowboarder B**

Go forward 4 squares
Make 1 right angle turn clockwise.
Go forward 3 squares.
Make 1 **right angle turn anticlockwise**.
Go forward 3 squares.
Make 1 **right angle turn anticlockwise**.
Go forward 1 square.
Make 1 right angle turn clockwise.
Go forward 2 squares.
Make 1 right angle turn clockwise.
Go forward 2 squares.

| | | | | | |
|---|---|---|---|---|---|
| | | | | | |
| | | | | | |
| | | | | | |
| | | | | | 🏁 |

_____

_____

_____

_____

_____

**Teacher's notes**

At the top of the page, children draw the route of snowboarder A and snowboarder B onto the race track above. They then put a ring around the directions which led the snowboarder to the flag. At the bottom of the page, children plan a course on the empty grid. They write directions for how to reach the finish line.

# Writing directions

Date: _____

Write directions in right angles

| Start on | Start on | Start on |
| --- | --- | --- |
| Go forward 3 squares | | |
| | | |
| | | |
| | | |
| | | |
| | | |
| | | |
| | | |
| | | |
| You have arrived on: | You have arrived on: | You have arrived on: |

**Teacher's notes**

Children use the grid at the top of the page to write directions from the given starting point to the given end point – Earth. Ensure the children realize that they do not need to write a direction in each box. When the children have written all three sets of directions, they swap with a partner to check the accuracy of each other's directions.

13

Date: _____

# Fruit 2s

## Counting in 2s

There are ☐ apples altogether.

There are ☐ pineapples altogether.

There are ☐ bananas altogether.

There are ☐ strawberries altogether.

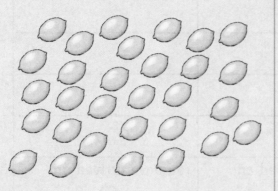

There are ☐ lemons altogether.

There are ☐ grapes altogether.

## Teacher's notes

Children look at each set of fruit and count them in twos, circling each set of two as they do so. They then write the total number underneath to complete each sentence.

# Half time halves and doubles

Date: _____

## Recall the multiplication and division facts for the 2 times table

$12 \div 2 = \boxed{\phantom{0}}$    **12**    $\boxed{\phantom{0}} \times 2 = 12$

$\boxed{\phantom{0}} \div 2 = \boxed{\phantom{0}}$    **18**    $\boxed{\phantom{0}} \times 2 = \boxed{\phantom{0}}$

$\boxed{\phantom{0}} \div 2 = \boxed{\phantom{0}}$    **16**    $\boxed{\phantom{0}} \times 2 = \boxed{\phantom{0}}$

$\boxed{\phantom{0}} \div 2 = \boxed{\phantom{0}}$    **24**    $\boxed{\phantom{0}} \times 2 = \boxed{\phantom{0}}$

$\boxed{\phantom{0}} \div 2 = \boxed{\phantom{0}}$    **20**    $\boxed{\phantom{0}} \times 2 = \boxed{\phantom{0}}$

**Teacher's notes**

Children look at the number on each footballer's shirt and then use it to complete the multiplication and division calculations in the nets on each side.

15

Date: _____

# 5s in a hive

## Count in steps of 5

There are ⬤ bees altogether.

There are ⬤ bees altogether.

There are ⬤ bees altogether.

There are ⬤ bees altogether.

There are ⬤ bees altogether.

There are ⬤ bees altogether.

**Teacher's notes**

Children look at each swarm of bees and count them in fives, circling each set of five as they do so. They then write the total number underneath to complete each sentence.

Date: _____

# Camping calculations

Recall the multiplication and division facts for the 5 times table

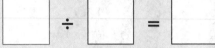

6 x 5 = ☐        ☐ ÷ ☐ = ☐

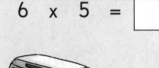

3 x 5 = ☐        ☐ ÷ ☐ = ☐

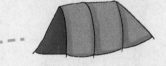

9 x 5 = ☐        ☐ ÷ ☐ = ☐

4 x 5 = ☐        ☐ ÷ ☐ = ☐

12 x 5 = ☐       ☐ ÷ ☐ = ☐

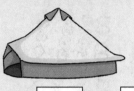

**Teacher's notes**

Children look at the multiplication calculation below each camper van and write the answer in the box. They then follow the trail that leads to a tent. They write a related division fact beneath the tent.

# How many beads?

## Counting in 10s

Date: _____

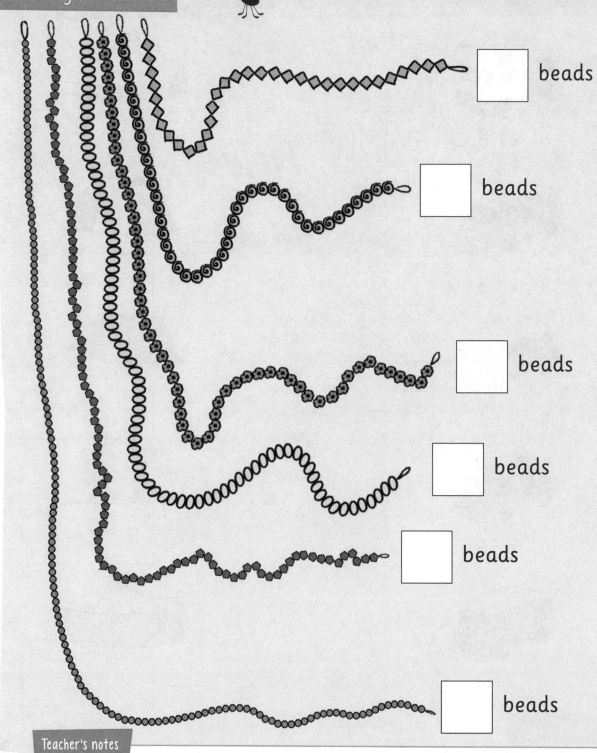

beads

beads

beads

beads

beads

beads

**Teacher's notes**

Children count how many beads there are in each necklace, making a mark after each set of ten beads. Then they write the total number of beads in the box.

# Ant hill 10s

Date: _____

Recall the multiplication and division facts for the 10 times table

**You will need:**
• coloured pencils

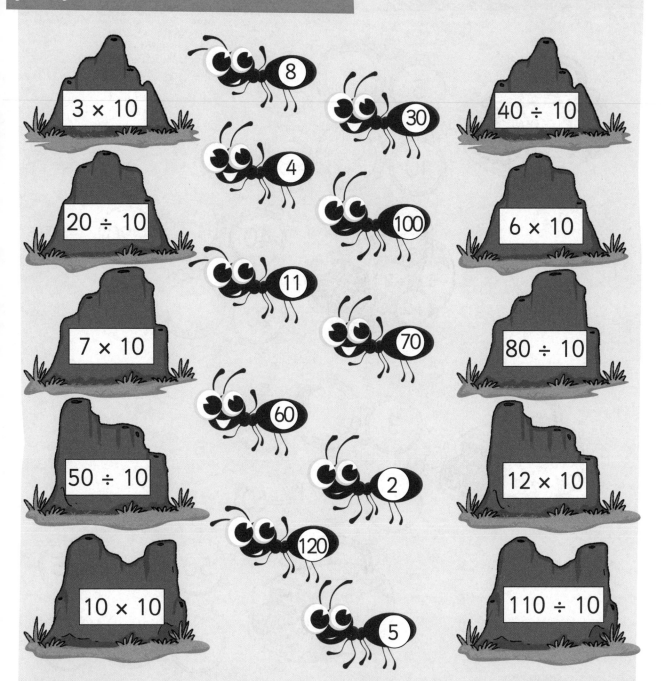

3 × 10

8

30

40 ÷ 10

20 ÷ 10

4

100

6 × 10

7 × 10

11

70

80 ÷ 10

50 ÷ 10

60

2

12 × 10

10 × 10

120

5

110 ÷ 10

**Teacher's notes**

Children look at each anthill and draw a line joining the multiplication or division calculation to the ant showing the correct answer.

# Bubble machines

Date: _____

Recall the multiplication and division facts for the 2, 5 and 10 times tables

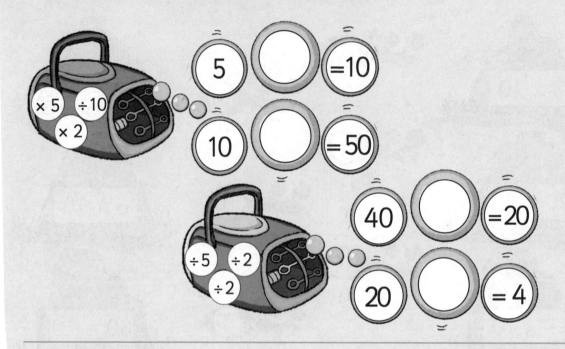

Date: _____

# Museum multiplication and division

Solve problems using the multiplication and division facts for the 2, 5 and 10 times tables

10p    2p    ☐ p    5p    ☐ p    ☐ p

---

 Caie buys 5 sweets.
He spends 25p.

☐ ◯ ☐ ◯ ☐

Each sweets costs ☐ p.

---

Rosa buys 2 ice-creams.
She spends 24p.

☐ ◯ ☐ ◯ ☐

Each ice-creams costs ☐ p.

---

 Evie buys 12 lollipops.

☐ ◯ ◯ ◯ ☐

She spends ☐ p.

---

 Cavan buys 8 dinosaurs.

☐ ◯ ☐ ◯ ☐

He spends ☐ p.

---

 Yasmin buys 5 notebooks.
She spends 50p.

☐ ◯ ☐ ◯ ☐

Each notebook cost ☐ p.

---

 Nye buys 6 pencils.

☐ ◯ ☐ ◯ ☐

He spends ☐ p.

---

## Teacher's notes

Children look at each word problem and work out the answer using multiplication or division.
For the division problems, they write the cost of each item on the label next to each one when they find the answer.

Date: _____

# Thermometer problems

## Solve problems involving temperature

## The temperature in Didsbury on a summer day.

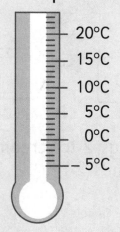

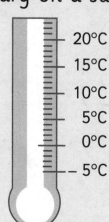

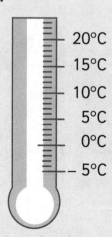

Morning: 7°C.

Afternoon: 13°C higher than the morning ☐ °C.

Evening: 5°C lower than the afternoon ☐ °C.

## The temperature in Didsbury on a winter day.

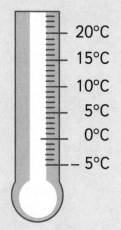

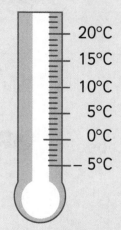

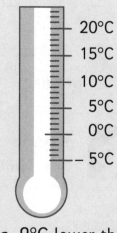

Morning: − 5°C.

Afternoon: 12°C higher than the morning ☐ °C.

Evening: 9°C lower than the afternoon ☐ °C.

# Width problems

Date: _____

## Compare widths by halving and doubling

Bradley wants to know the widths of all his books. Can you help him find out?

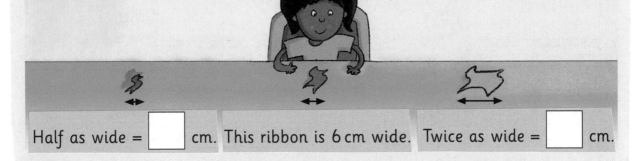

Half as wide = [ ] cm.  This book is 24 cm wide.  Twice as wide = [ ] cm.

Carly wants to know the widths of all her ribbons. Can you help her find out?

Half as wide = [ ] cm.  This ribbon is 6 cm wide.  Twice as wide = [ ] cm.

Bobby wants to know the widths of the strips of paper. Can you help him find out?

Half as wide = [ ] cm.  This strip of paper is 50 cm wide.  Twice as wide = [ ] cm.

**Teacher's notes**

Children work out the widths of the objects above by halving or doubling the width of the middle object.

# Mass problems

Compare mass by halving and doubling

Date: _____

Recipe for 8 people:
Ingredients:
300 g flour
200 g sugar
200 g butter
150 g chocolate
4 eggs

Recipe for 4 people:

| | flour |
| --- | --- |
| | sugar |
| | butter |
| | chocolate |
| | eggs |

Recipe for 16 people:

| | flour |
| --- | --- |
| | sugar |
| | butter |
| | chocolate |
| | eggs |

To bake the cake for 4 people and the cake for 16 people, the cook will need:

☐ flour  ☐ sugar  ☐ butter  ☐ chocolate  ☐ eggs

Teacher's notes

Children work out how much of each ingredient needed to bake for four people and sixteen people. They do this by halving and doubling the ingredients for eight people. Then they find the total of the amounts needed to bake the cake for four people and the cake for sixteen people.

Date: _____

# Capacity and volume problems

## Solve problems involving capacity and volume

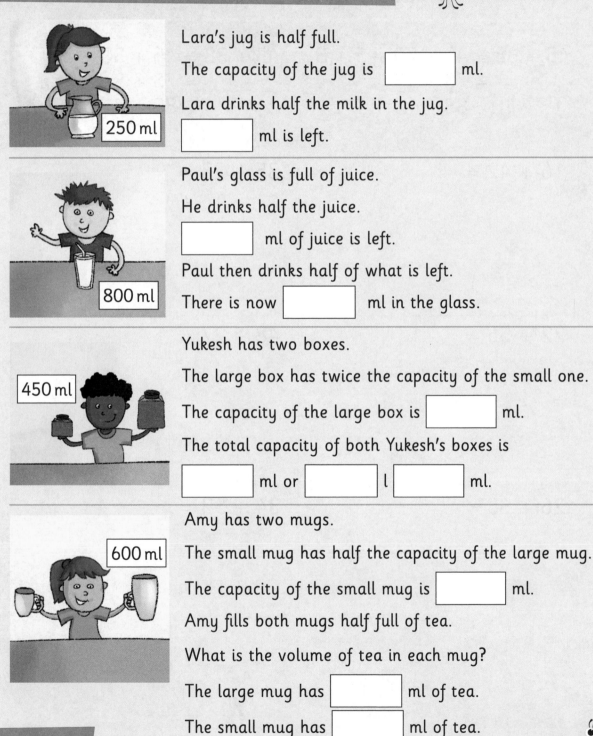

Lara's jug is half full.

The capacity of the jug is [ ] ml.

Lara drinks half the milk in the jug.

[ ] ml is left.

250 ml

---

Paul's glass is full of juice.

He drinks half the juice.

[ ] ml of juice is left.

Paul then drinks half of what is left.

There is now [ ] ml in the glass.

800 ml

---

Yukesh has two boxes.

The large box has twice the capacity of the small one.

The capacity of the large box is [ ] ml.

The total capacity of both Yukesh's boxes is

[ ] ml or [ ] l [ ] ml.

450 ml

---

Amy has two mugs.

600 ml

The small mug has half the capacity of the large mug.

The capacity of the small mug is [ ] ml.

Amy fills both mugs half full of tea.

What is the volume of tea in each mug?

The large mug has [ ] ml of tea.

The small mug has [ ] ml of tea.

Teacher's notes

Children use the information in the pictures to help them solve the problems.

25

# Using place value to add

Date: _____

L·O Add numbers using partitioning

| | |
|---|---|
| 45 + 38 = 40 + 30 + 5 + 8 <br> = 70 + 13 <br> = 83 | 45 + 38 = 45 + 30 + 8 <br> = 75 + 8 <br> = 83 |

| | |
|---|---|
| 16 + 42 = | 35 + 23 = |
| 22 + 56 = | 48 + 27 = |
| 26 + 65 = | 34 + 59 = |

Teacher's notes

Children add each pair of numbers using their preferred method from the two examples given.

26

Date: _____

# Problems at the park

## Solve word problems

Alfie saw 24 ducks and 18 geese on the pond. How many birds did he see altogether?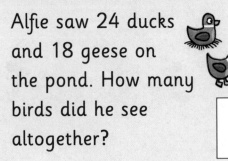

15 children and 28 adults went to the park for a party picnic. How many people were at the picnic?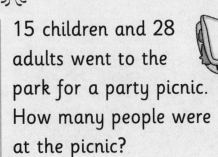

The ice-cream man sold 45 cones and 36 ice lollies. What is the total number of items he sold?

There are 66 people playing football and 28 people playing netball in the park. How many people are playing sport in the park?

### Teacher's notes

Children choose their own preferred method for solving each of the problems. They use the space below each problem for working out.

Date: _____

# Using place value to subtract

## Subtract numbers using partitioning

$$86 - 23 = 86 - 20 - 3$$
$$= 66 - 3$$
$$= 63$$

| | |
|---|---|
| 36 – 12 = | 72 – 45 = |
| 65 – 43 = | 54 – 38 = |
| 49 – 27 = | 93 – 64 = |

**Teacher's notes**

The three questions on the left of the page do not require the children to cross a tens boundary.
The three questions on the right of the page do involve crossing a tens boundary.

Date: _____

# Problems on the move

Solve word problems

There were 83 passengers on a boat. 38 got off. How many are left on the boat?

A bus has 75 passengers. 56 of them are sitting down. How many are standing?

95 cyclists start a race. 17 of them are too tired to finish. How many finish the race?

There are 73 bus drivers. 26 are men. How many are women?

Teacher's notes

Children choose their own preferred method for solving each of the problems using the space at the bottom of each problem for working out.

Date: _____

# Written addition

Add two 2-digit numbers using the expanded written method

23 + 38 =

20 + 3
30 + 8
_____
50 + 11 = 61
_____

$$
\begin{array}{r}
23 \\
+38 \\
\hline
11 \\
50 \\
\hline
61
\end{array}
$$

| 26 + 17 = | 34 + 28 = |
|---|---|
| 55 + 27 = | 43 + 38 = |
| 28 + 64 = | 36 + 57 = |

Date: _____

# Written subtraction

Subtract two 2-digit numbers using the written method

$$\begin{array}{r} 46 \\ -\ 25 \\ \hline 21 \end{array}$$

| | |
|---|---|
| 58 – 32 = | 47 – 13 = |
| 65 – 42 = | 57 – 24 = |
| 78 – 55 = | 96 – 73 = |

**Teacher's notes**

Children subtract each pair of numbers using the written method. Note that each of these calculations does not require decomposition.

Date: _____

# Zoo problems

The snakes ate 48 mice on Saturday and 44 mice on Sunday. How many mice did they eat altogether at the weekend?

The keeper gives the monkeys 78 bananas. They eat 66 of them. How many bananas are left?

There are 45 penguins in the zoo and 22 of them are swimming. How many are not swimming?

There are 37 green parrots and 45 red parrots. How many parrots are there in total?

Date: _____

# Castle problems

Solve addition and subtraction problems using mental and written methods

The castle has 19 red flags and 27 yellow flags. How many flags are there in total?

67 people live in the castle. 24 of them go out for the day. How many people are still in the castle?

The castle has 36 windows and 41 arrow slits. How many windows and arrow slits are there altogether?

63 candles were burning in the castle. 25 of them went out. How many candles are still burning?

**Teacher's notes**

Children use a mental or written method to solve each word problem using the space at the bottom of each problem for any working out.

Date: _____

# Class 2T

Interpret a block diagram

## Class 2T Birth Months

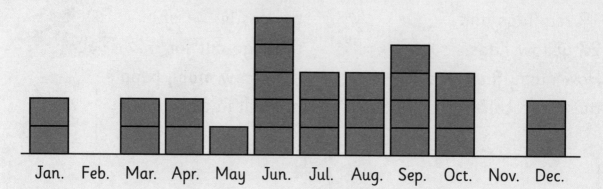

Jan.  Feb.  Mar.  Apr.  May  Jun.  Jul.  Aug.  Sep.  Oct.  Nov.  Dec.

**Key** ☐ = 1 child

Use the block diagram to answer these questions.

There are ☐ children in Class 2T.

☐ is the month when most children were born.

☐ and ☐ are

the months when fewest children were born.

3 children were born in ☐,

☐ and ☐.

No children were born in [_____] and [_____] .

Summer-born children are born in June, July and August.

There are [ ] summer-born children in Class 2T.

There are [ ] winter-born children in Class 2T.

Complete the frequency table for each month.

| Jan. | Feb. | Mar. | Apr. | May | Jun. | Jul. | Aug. | Sep. | Oct. | Nov. | Dec. |
|------|------|------|------|-----|------|------|------|------|------|------|------|
|      |      |      |      |     |      |      |      |      |      |      |      |

Think of your own question which can be answered from the block diagram. Write the question and the answer.

Teacher's notes

The block diagram shows the birth months for children in Class 2T. Each block represents one child. Children use the diagram to complete the sentences. You may need to prompt them to think about which are the "winter" months. The focus is on birth month so that those children who do not celebrate birthdays are included. Children complete the frequency table at the bottom of this page by counting the blocks in each month on the block diagram at the top of page 34 then they think of their own question and write its answer in the space below.

# Dice diagram

Date: _____

• Construct and interpret a block diagram
• Answer questions about a block diagram

**You will need:**
• 2 × 1–6 dice
• coloured pencils

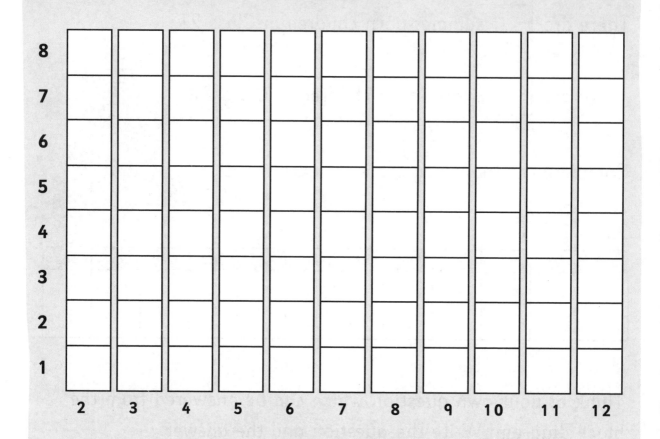

Each time you roll the dice, you colour in the total. So the columns with the most blocks will be the totals made most often.

## After 10 rolls...

I have made these totals most often: ☐.

I have not made these totals: ☐.

## After 10 more rolls...

I have made this total (or totals) most often: [_____].

I have made these new totals: [_____].

I have not made these totals: [_____].

Are your answers the same after 20 throws and after 30

throws? [_____].

---

Make up a question which can be answered from the Block Diagram.

[                                                            ]

What is the answer to your question?

[                                                            ]

**Teacher's notes**

Children roll the two dice and add the numbers together. They then colour in a square for the total, starting from the bottom of a column and repeat 10 times. They then use the block diagram to answer the first set of questions. They roll the dice 10 more times and answer the second set of questions. Some children will find it useful to make a tally mark each time they roll and total the dice to keep track of what they are doing. Children who need more support should use one dice.

# Lost!

Date: _____

## Find out information from a pictogram

In a box of shapes, there should be six shapes in each colour – a circle, triangle, square, rectangle, pentagon and hexagon. Some children were asked to check the shapes were all there. They laid the shapes out in a pictogram.

**You will need:**
- coloured pencils
- Resource 6: 2-D shapes (circle, triangle, square, rectangle, pentagon and hexagon)

| | | | | | | |
|---|---|---|---|---|---|---|
| Red | circle | triangle | rectangle | pentagon | | |
| Yellow | pentagon | square | triangle | hexagon | | |
| Green | square | hexagon | pentagon | rectangle | circle | |
| Blue | hexagon | rectangle | triangle | square | | |
| Orange | triangle | square | rectangle | circle | hexagon | |
| Black | rectangle | hexagon | circle | triangle | pentagon | square |

One green shape is missing.

It is a [_____].

Two red shapes are missing.

They are a [_____] and a [_____].

Two yellow shapes are missing.

They are a [_____] and a [_____].

Two blue shapes are missing.

They are a [_____] and a [_____].

One orange shape is missing.

It is a [_____].

---

After lots of searching, the missing shapes are found.

Add them to the pictogram.

Teacher's notes

Each row should have six shapes in each colour – a circle, triangle, square, rectangle, pentagon and hexagon. Children use the information in the pictogram to identify the missing shapes and answer the questions.

# Our chickens

Date: _____

Draw a pictogram or block diagram to make it easier to answer questions about the data

**You will need:**
- coloured pencils

| | Number of eggs collected | | | | | |
|---|---|---|---|---|---|---|
| | Week 1 | Week 2 | Week 3 | Week 4 | Week 5 | Week 6 |
| Monday | 2 | 3 | 2 | 3 | 2 | 2 |
| Tuesday | 3 | 3 | 4 | 3 | 3 | 3 |
| Wednesday | 3 | 4 | 4 | 3 | 3 | 3 |
| Thursday | 3 | 3 | 4 | 2 | 5 | 3 |
| Friday | 2 | 5 | 3 | 3 | 2 | 4 |
| Saturday | 1 | 1 | 2 | 1 | 2 | 1 |
| Sunday | 2 | 2 | 1 | 2 | 1 | 2 |

**Key** ⬭ = 2 eggs,  🥚 = 1 egg

| | | | | | | | | | | |
|---|---|---|---|---|---|---|---|---|---|---|
| M | | | | | | | | | | |
| T | | | | | | | | | | |
| W | | | | | | | | | | |
| T | | | | | | | | | | |
| F | | | | | | | | | | |
| S | | | | | | | | | | |
| S | | | | | | | | | | |

| | Monday | Tuesday | Wednesday | Thursday | Friday | Saturday | Sunday |
|---|---|---|---|---|---|---|---|
| 20 | | | | | | | |
| 18 | | | | | | | |
| 16 | | | | | | | |
| 14 | | | | | | | |
| 12 | | | | | | | |
| 10 | | | | | | | |
| 8 | | | | | | | |
| 6 | | | | | | | |
| 4 | | | | | | | |
| 2 | | | | | | | |

The chickens laid the most eggs on ⬚.

The chickens laid the fewest eggs on ⬚.

Teacher's notes

Children complete the pictogram on page 40 by drawing an egg or half an egg in each space. Each egg represents 2 eggs laid, with half an egg representing one egg laid. Children then complete the block block diagram at the top of this page by colouring one square for 2 eggs or half a square for a single egg. The block diagram is already labelled in twos.

# Shopping multiples

Date: _____

Count in 2s, 5s and 10s and recognise
multiples of 2, 5 and 10

Multiples of 2 | Multiples of 5 | Multiples of 10

**Teacher's notes**

Children decide whether the price on each item is a multiple of two, five or ten. They should write each
number on the appropriate shopping receipt. Some prices will go on more than one receipt.

# Apple arrays

**Date:** _____

Calculate multiplication and division facts for the 2, 5 and 10 times tables

☐ × ☐ = ☐     ☐ × ☐ = ☐

☐ ÷ ☐ = ☐     ☐ ÷ ☐ = ☐

☐ × ☐ = ☐     ☐ × ☐ = ☐

☐ ÷ ☐ = ☐     ☐ ÷ ☐ = ☐

☐ × ☐ = ☐     ☐ × ☐ = ☐

☐ ÷ ☐ = ☐     ☐ ÷ ☐ = ☐

☐ × ☐ = ☐     ☐ × ☐ = ☐

☐ ÷ ☐ = ☐     ☐ ÷ ☐ = ☐

☐ × ☐ = ☐     ☐ × ☐ = ☐

☐ ÷ ☐ = ☐     ☐ ÷ ☐ = ☐

☐ × ☐ = ☐     ☐ × ☐ = ☐

☐ ÷ ☐ = ☐     ☐ ÷ ☐ = ☐

**Teacher's notes**

Children look at each array of apples and find the two multiplication and two division facts for each array.

43

# Number problems

**Date:** _____

## Solve multiplication and division problems

There are 7 trees in the field. There are 5 birds in each tree.

☐ ◯ ☐ ◯ ☐

There are ☐ birds in the trees.

---

Amber has 24 flowers. She puts them into 2 vases.

☐ ◯ ☐ ◯ ☐

She puts ☐ flowers into each vase.

---

Ellis has 5 shelves in his room. Altogether he has 40 books.

☐ ◯ ☐ ◯ ☐

Ellis has ☐ books on each shelf.

---

Leon bakes 12 cakes. He puts 5 chocolate buttons on each one.

☐ ◯ ☐ ◯ ☐

Leon uses ☐ chocolate buttons.

---

Min has 2 toy boxes. She tidies away 11 games into each one.

☐ ◯ ☐ ◯ ☐

Min has ☐ games altogether.

---

There are 30 pencils in the class. They are shared equally between 5 pots.

☐ ◯ ☐ ◯ ☐

There are ☐ pencils in each pot.

---

**Teacher's notes**

Children look at each word problem and decide which operation to use to solve it. Then they write the appropriate calculation in the spaces provided and fill in the answer to complete each sentence.

Date: _____

# What's the problem?

Solve problems using the multiplication and division facts for the 2, 5 and 10 times tables

Erin puts 16 cars into toy boxes. There are 2 toy boxes. How many cars does Erin put in each toy box?

☐ ◯ ☐ ◯ ☐

Erin puts ☐ cars in each toy box.

Caie bakes 35 chocolate cookies. He shares these between 5 people. How many cookies do they have each?

☐ ◯ ☐ ◯ ☐

They have ☐ cookies each.

Ms Green shared 100 kg of cherries between 10 crates. How many kg in each crate?

☐ ◯ ☐ ◯ ☐

There are ☐ kg in each crate.

Mr Pott sold 9 bunches of roses for £5 each. How much money did he make?

☐ ◯ ☐ ◯ ☐

Mr Pott made £ ☐ .

Malkeet buys 9 pencils for 10p each. How much does he spend?

☐ ◯ ☐ ◯ ☐

Malkeet spends ☐ p.

Amina puts 12 flowers into each vase. She has 2 vases. How many flowers does she have altogether?

☐ ◯ ☐ ◯ ☐

Amina has ☐ flowers altogether.

Teacher's notes

Children look at each word problem and decide which operation to use to solve it. Then they write the appropriate calculation in the spaces provided and fill in the answer to complete each sentence.

45

# Fraction wall

Date: _____

Mark fractions on a number line to compare them

**You will need:**
• ruler

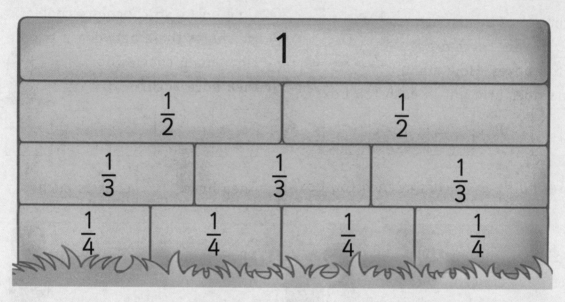

0 ———————————————————————————————— 1

Which is bigger, $\frac{1}{4}$ or $\frac{1}{3}$? ☐

Which is smaller, $\frac{3}{4}$ or $\frac{2}{3}$? ☐

Write a fraction that is between $\frac{1}{4}$ and $\frac{1}{2}$: ☐

Write a fraction that is between $\frac{1}{3}$ and $\frac{2}{3}$: ☐

**Teacher's notes**

Children use a ruler to mark $\frac{1}{2}$, $\frac{1}{4}$, $\frac{3}{4}$, $\frac{1}{3}$ and $\frac{2}{3}$ on the number line below the fraction wall. They can answer the questions below using the number line or fraction wall.

# Fraction washing lines

Date: _____

Draw the fraction washing on the washing line in the correct place

**You will need:**
- coloured pencils

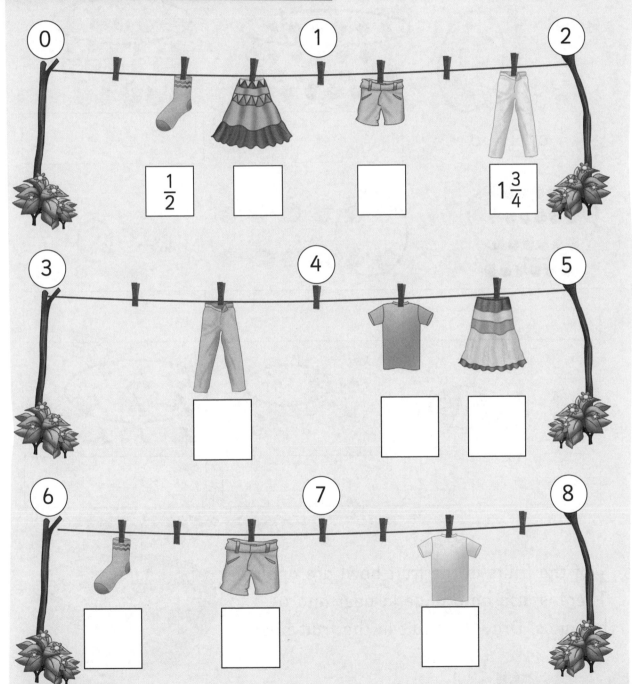

0    1    2

$\frac{1}{2}$    ☐    ☐    $1\frac{3}{4}$

3    4    5

6    7    8

**Teacher's notes**

Children look at each piece of clothing on the washing lines and write down, as a fraction, how far along each piece of line the clothing is hanging.

47

# Fruit fractions

**Recognise and find fractions of a set of objects**

Date: _____

**You will need:**
- coloured pencils

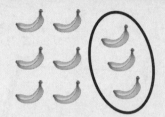

$$\frac{1}{3} \text{ of } 9 = 3$$

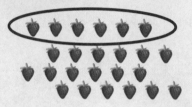

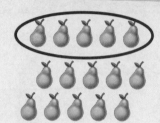

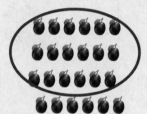

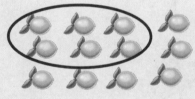

$\frac{1}{4}$ of the fruits in the fruit bowl are apples. There is also an orange, a pear and 4 bananas. Draw the fruit in the fruit bowl.

**Teacher's notes**

Children work out what fraction of the whole is ringed then write the matching fraction number sentence. They use their knowledge of fractions to draw the correct fruit in the bowl at the bottom of the page.

48

# Fraction problems

Date: _____

## Solve problems involving fractions

There are 12 pages in my book.

I have read $\frac{1}{4}$ of it.

I have ⬜ pages left to read.

---

I have 10 sweets. I give you half.

I have given you ⬜ sweets.

---

The toy I want is half price today.

It now costs £ ⬜ .

 £8

---

I ate one third of the bowl of cherries.

If I ate 10 cherries, there were ⬜ in

the bowl to start with.

---

The pizza was cut into 8 equal slices.

Tamim ate one quarter of the pizza.

She ate ⬜ slices.

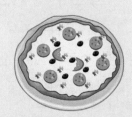

---

# How many minutes?

**Date:** _____

Tell and draw hands on clocks to show the time to five minutes

**You will need:**
- small clock (per child)

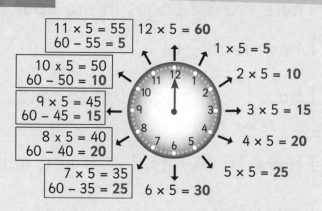

| 20 | to | 5 |

| | to | |

| | to | |

| | to | |

| 25 | to | 5 |

| 10 | to | 8 |

| 5 | to | 3 |

| 20 | to | 1 |

Quarter to 4 = [   ] minutes before 4 o'clock = 45 minutes after 3 o'clock.

Quarter to [   ] = [   ] minutes before 8 o'clock = 45 minutes after 7 o'clock.

**Teacher's notes**

Children draw times on the clock faces to match the written time or write the time shown on the clock face. They then answer some questions to revise the meaning of 'quarter to'.

# Time differences

Date: _____

Tell and write the time to 5 minutes

**You will need:**
• a small clock

| $\frac{1}{4}$ past 10 |  | 20 minutes later |  |

| |  | 5 minutes later |  |

| |  | 55 minutes later |  |

| | | 10 minutes later | |

| | | 25 minutes later |  |

**Teacher's notes**

For each row of clocks, children think of a time. They write the time in the box and draw the hands on the first clock to match. They then read the label and draw the hands on the second clock to show the new time.

# My day

Date: _____

### Know the number of hours in a day

**You will need:**
- coloured pencils

| Key | |
|---|---|
| asleep | blue |
| eating | |
| | |
| | |
| | |
| | |
| | |
| | |
| | |

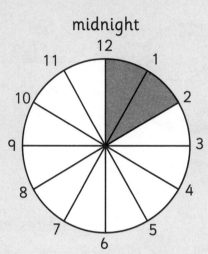

midnight

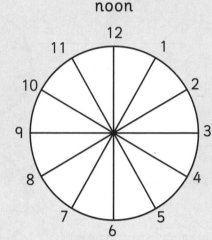

noon

How many hours were you asleep?

Other than sleeping, what did you do most of the time?

What did you spend the least amount of time doing?

What was your favourite thing that you did?

How long did you spend doing it?

**Teacher's notes**

Each segment of the clock represents 1 hour. The first clock starts at midnight, the second one at noon. Children choose a day to focus on and colour in the hours to represent what they were doing at that time on that day, completing the key at the same time. Hour segments could be split into half or quarter hours with a line from the edge of the circle to the middle. Children answer the questions about their day.

Date: _____

# Trip to the zoo

Solve problems relating to time

**You will need:**
• clock
• time number line

## Zoo trip timetable

• Walk to the station takes 20 minutes.
• Meet at station at quarter to 10.
• Train leaves 10 past 10.
• Journey takes 25 minutes.
• Walk to zoo takes 10 minutes.
• Picnic lunch at 12 noon for half an hour.
• Meet at the elephants at 20 past 4.
• Walk to the station takes 10 minutes.
• Train leaves at 20 to 5.
• Journey takes 35 minutes.

Leave home by ☐ to get to the station for quarter to 10.

You arrive at the zoo at ☐ .

You spend ☐ at the zoo in the morning.

You spend ☐ at the zoo in the afternoon.

You arrive back at your home station at ☐ .

**Teacher's notes**

Children read the timetable then use it to help them answer the questions. Some children may find a clock or time number line useful.

# Maths facts

## Number and place value

```
0  1  2  3  4  5  6  7  8  9  10  11  12  13  14  15  16  17  18  19  20
```

| 100 | 200 | 300 | 400 | 500 | 600 | 700 | 800 | 900 |
|-----|-----|-----|-----|-----|-----|-----|-----|-----|
| 10  | 20  | 30  | 40  | 50  | 60  | 70  | 80  | 90  |
| 1   | 2   | 3   | 4   | 5   | 6   | 7   | 8   | 9   |

| 1  | 2  | 3  | 4  | 5  | 6  | 7  | 8  | 9  | 10  |
|----|----|----|----|----|----|----|----|----|-----|
| 11 | 12 | 13 | 14 | 15 | 16 | 17 | 18 | 19 | 20  |
| 21 | 22 | 23 | 24 | 25 | 26 | 27 | 28 | 29 | 30  |
| 31 | 32 | 33 | 34 | 35 | 36 | 37 | 38 | 39 | 40  |
| 41 | 42 | 43 | 44 | 45 | 46 | 47 | 48 | 49 | 50  |
| 51 | 52 | 53 | 54 | 55 | 56 | 57 | 58 | 59 | 60  |
| 61 | 62 | 63 | 64 | 65 | 66 | 67 | 68 | 69 | 70  |
| 71 | 72 | 73 | 74 | 75 | 76 | 77 | 78 | 79 | 80  |
| 81 | 82 | 83 | 84 | 85 | 86 | 87 | 88 | 89 | 90  |
| 91 | 92 | 93 | 94 | 95 | 96 | 97 | 98 | 99 | 100 |

## Fractions

Half: $\frac{1}{2}$

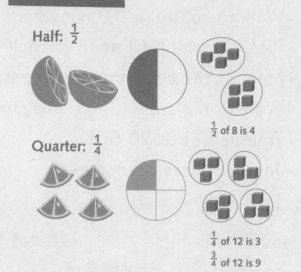

$\frac{1}{2}$ of 8 is 4

Quarter: $\frac{1}{4}$

$\frac{1}{4}$ of 12 is 3

$\frac{3}{4}$ of 12 is 9

## Addition and subtraction

| +  | 0  | 1  | 2  | 3  | 4  | 5  | 6  | 7  | 8  | 9  | 10 |
|----|----|----|----|----|----|----|----|----|----|----|----|
| 0  | 0  | 1  | 2  | 3  | 4  | 5  | 6  | 7  | 8  | 9  | 10 |
| 1  | 1  | 2  | 3  | 4  | 5  | 6  | 7  | 8  | 9  | 10 | 11 |
| 2  | 2  | 3  | 4  | 5  | 6  | 7  | 8  | 9  | 10 | 11 | 12 |
| 3  | 3  | 4  | 5  | 6  | 7  | 8  | 9  | 10 | 11 | 12 | 13 |
| 4  | 4  | 5  | 6  | 7  | 8  | 9  | 10 | 11 | 12 | 13 | 14 |
| 5  | 5  | 6  | 7  | 8  | 9  | 10 | 11 | 12 | 13 | 14 | 15 |
| 6  | 6  | 7  | 8  | 9  | 10 | 11 | 12 | 13 | 14 | 15 | 16 |
| 7  | 7  | 8  | 9  | 10 | 11 | 12 | 13 | 14 | 15 | 16 | 17 |
| 8  | 8  | 9  | 10 | 11 | 12 | 13 | 14 | 15 | 16 | 17 | 18 |
| 9  | 9  | 10 | 11 | 12 | 13 | 14 | 15 | 16 | 17 | 18 | 19 |
| 10 | 10 | 11 | 12 | 13 | 14 | 15 | 16 | 17 | 18 | 19 | 20 |

| +  | 11 | 12 | 13 | 14 | 15 | 16 | 17 | 18 | 19 | 20 |
|----|----|----|----|----|----|----|----|----|----|----|
| 0  | 11 | 12 | 13 | 14 | 15 | 16 | 17 | 18 | 19 | 20 |
| 1  | 12 | 13 | 14 | 15 | 16 | 17 | 18 | 19 | 20 |    |
| 2  | 13 | 14 | 15 | 16 | 17 | 18 | 19 | 20 |    |    |
| 3  | 14 | 15 | 16 | 17 | 18 | 19 | 20 |    |    |    |
| 4  | 15 | 16 | 17 | 18 | 19 | 20 |    |    |    |    |
| 5  | 16 | 17 | 18 | 19 | 20 |    |    |    |    |    |
| 6  | 17 | 18 | 19 | 20 |    |    |    |    |    |    |
| 7  | 18 | 19 | 20 |    |    |    |    |    |    |    |
| 8  | 19 | 20 |    |    |    |    |    |    |    |    |
| 9  | 20 |    |    |    |    |    |    |    |    |    |

# Multiplication and division

| × | 2 | 5 | 10 |
|---|---|---|---|
| 1 | 2 | 5 | 10 |
| 2 | 4 | 10 | 20 |
| 3 | 6 | 15 | 30 |
| 4 | 8 | 20 | 40 |
| 5 | 10 | 25 | 50 |
| 6 | 12 | 30 | 60 |
| 7 | 14 | 35 | 70 |
| 8 | 16 | 40 | 80 |
| 9 | 18 | 45 | 90 |
| 10 | 20 | 50 | 100 |
| 11 | 22 | 55 | 110 |
| 12 | 24 | 60 | 120 |

## Multiples of 2

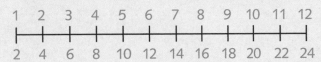

## Multiples of 5

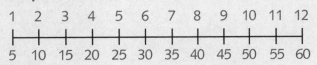

## Multiples of 10

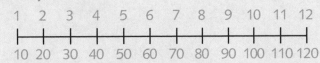

# Measurement (time)

**20 past 7**   **$\frac{1}{4}$ to 4**

# Position and direction

clockwise

$\frac{1}{4}$ turn    $\frac{1}{2}$ turn    $\frac{3}{4}$ turn

anti-clockwise

$\frac{1}{4}$ turn    $\frac{1}{2}$ turn    $\frac{3}{4}$ turn

# Properties of shapes

## 2-D shapes

circle   triangle   square   rectangle   pentagon   hexagon   octagon

## 3-D shapes

cube   cuboid   cone   cylinder   sphere   triangular-based pyramid   square-based pyramid